SERMON OUTLINES
on

Conversations
of Christ

Charles R. Wood

kregel
PUBLICATIONS

Grand Rapids, MI 49501

Contents

Introduction

It seems as if Jesus was always talking to and with people. Sometimes, as with the discourse on the mountain at the opening of His ministry, He spoke to large groups of people; other times He engaged a single person in conversation. In many of His conversations that have been recorded, He spoke within the context of His own band of followers, but He also was constantly engaged by and with the Pharisees.

He considered worthy of conversation anyone who wished to speak with Him.

Some of the most profound truths that He uttered were spoken in the course of these conversations. He spoke uniformly of spiritual things, He regularly propounded eternal principles in the simplest of settings, and as the conversations unfolded, He demonstrated an incredible level of knowledge of what was really in the hearts of those with whom He spoke. His conversations should be—and are—a rich source of information about what He is really like, this One after whom we are to pattern our lives.

The messages included in this book have been somewhat arbitrarily and randomly selected from the vast store of those available in the Gospels. The unifying theme in the selection, though, is the practicality of the teaching involved in each exchange. The very fact that He spoke so readily with such a wide array of people challenges our tendency to communicate primarily with those whom we are most comfortable. No one was "beneath His dignity" or outside the pale of His compassion. He had a dimension that we do not possess in that His divine nature gave Him insights beyond anything we can know. This measure of omniscience, however, is not sufficient to detract from the pattern provided to His modern followers.

Read and study the text; the sermons in this book should greatly facilitate (and abbreviate) that process. Be sure you understand the statements, their movements, and the ways in which they relate to each other. Make the message your own, even if you use the outline exactly as printed on the page. Allow the Scripture to burn into your heart, and preach with the passion thus created.

May God grant you, the user of these messages, the same joy and fruitfulness that He graciously gave to this preacher when they were originally presented at different times during a half-century of preaching.

CHARLES R. WOOD

The Conversations of Christ that Didn't Involve a Miracle

Introduction:

It is amazing to note the amount of space the Gospels devote to Christ's conversations with a wide variety of people. Principles emerge from virtually every one of His conversations, and general principles recur in almost every situation.

I. **He Talked with People "on the Way" or "as He Was Going Along"**
    A. No set time or "meetings"
    B. We tend to compartmentalize our spiritual activities (e.g., "soul-winning" time)
    C. He walked slowly through the crowd and was always "on duty"

II. **He Always Had Time for Individuals**
    A. The maniac of Gadara is a prime illustration (Jesus crossed the lake just to deal with one individual)
    B. The proportion of His ministry invested in individuals is amazing
    C. Some of His ministry to the crowd arose, in fact, from individual encounters

III. **He Talked with Anyone Who Would Talk with Him**
    A. He never discriminated against anyone
    B. He was always accepting of the people He encountered
    C. He spoke with quite a cast of characters

IV. **He Gave Each Person to Whom He Spoke His Full Attention**
    A. He did nothing else when talking with them
    B. We tend to be distracted, to interrupt, to play "can you top this"
    C. We are often so busy framing our answers that we miss what people are saying or seeking

V. **He Listened as Well as Talked (Note His Use of Questions)**
    A. He saw and sensed the needs of people
    B. Doubtlessly, He did what we often can't do; He allowed silence
    C. He often "cut to the chase" in a way we can't

VI. He Treated Sincerity Seriously but Never Had Time for Hypocrisy
A. He must have known the young ruler would not respond
B. He was almost uniformly kind
C. The only exception to His kindness was when he dealt with the Pharisees

VII. He Never Argued or Debated with People
A. He never debated
B. He never went far with people who merely wanted to argue
C. He was always willing to discuss

VIII. He Didn't Get Involved in Judgmentalism
A. It was not part of His mission to judge
B. He knew the final count would not be in until eternity
C. He postponed judgment to its proper place—later

IX. He Didn't "Force the Issue" with People
A. He allowed people great freedom
B. The "cast of characters" represented a broad spectrum (from a young ruler to the men who brought an adulterous woman)
C. He never tried to trap or "sell" people

X. He Expected the Best of People
A. Because He saw the best in us, He could accept the worst in us
B. God never looks at your past to determine your future
C. He didn't put people on probation

XI. He Saw Salvation as an Event but Evangelism as a Process
A. There is no record that Nicodemus made a decision in John 3, but he shows up later as a believer
B. He made little effort to "close each deal"
C. We should always contribute toward the process, as we never know what the final outcome may be

XII. He Gave of Himself to Others
A. He gave everyone His best
B. He was wearied because He gave everyone everything He had
C. We view people in terms of our needs and agendas, but He didn't

Conclusion:

There is so much for us to learn from the ways in which Christ conversed with and treated people. We have a tendency to use people; He never did that. If ministry is all about people—and it is—then we need to pattern ours after His.

Some Words About Belief and Unbelief
Mark 9:14–29

Introduction:

This is an interesting story—this man with a demon-possessed son. Faith is so essential to Christianity that the Bible is filled with the theme. Faith, here, is addressed with a really crucial verse.

I. **The Measure of the Matter**
   A. The need was genuine
      1. The boy was demon possessed
      2. The possession was terrible (vv. 18, 21–22)
   B. The situation was desperate
      1. The man had done all he could do
      2. He had doubtlessly exhausted all the doctors
      3. He had likely gone to anyone who claimed the ability to heal
      4. He had now found the disciples powerless
   C. The plea was earnest
      1. It was made with tears (v. 24)
      2. It came from a desperate heart
   D. The faith was small
      1. The man had enough to get him there
      2. His own admission was that of small faith
   E. The success was complete
      1. There was a battle
      2. The boy was restored to normal life

II. **The Meaning of the Matter: "Lord, I believe; help thou mine unbelief"**

   These words could mean many things.
   A. Lord, I believe, but there is still much unbelief in me
      1. We all have to say that
      2. Even the person of the greatest faith among us must admit this
   B. Lord, I believe you can; help me to believe you will
      1. Most of us have no question about His ability
      2. Our problems center on His willingness and thus on our worthiness
   C. Lord, I believe you can, but I have tremendous trouble understanding how
      1. I don't really need to know, but I want to
      2. It is much more difficult to believe what one cannot understand

D. Lord, I believe, but my faith is ever so weak
   1. This is incredibly common
   2. He has done so much for us, but we still doubt

III. **The Message of the Matter**
A. Belief and unbelief can coexist
   1. We can have mixed signals at the same time and on the same thing
   2. We can believe on one thing while doubting another
B. Unbelief is not eradicated because I say, "I believe"
   1. One instance of triumphant faith does not settle the issue forever
   2. Saying it doesn't really "get it done"
C. Belief is not meaningless because there is a measure of unbelief present
   1. We are sometimes harsher on ourselves than He is
   2. Even a small measure of belief tends to create more
D. Belief is a growing thing that always has room for expansion
   1. No one reaches the pinnacle of faith
   2. One good thing about problems, they provide space for development of greater faith
E. Unbelief can be helped by turning it to the Lord
   1. The man prayed for help with his unbelief
   2. We can confess ours and ask for help as it is sin and should be treated that way
F. God will reward even the smallest amount of faith
   1. There was a real mixture here
   2. The man's faith was defective at best
   3. He got what he desired

Conclusion:
Don't despair over your lack of faith. Use what you have. Confess your lack. Seek God's help. We can all accomplish more than we do.

He Said, "No Longer Lonely"
John 16:5–15

Introduction:
There is a difference between being alone and being lonely. The fisherman is alone but not lonely. The widow is surrounded by family but is lonely. We all feel lonely at times, but we need not suffer from loneliness. The songwriter said, "You'll never walk alone" (Richard Rodgers and Oscar Hammerstein II, "You'll Never Walk Alone," 1945). The Bible offers us something better.

I.   **The Disciples' Anguish (vv. 5–6)**
   A. He told them He was going to leave them (14:2)
   B. They were terribly upset by that news
      1. None asks, "Where are you going?" All were too interested in the personal effects of His departure
      2. They were overflowing with sorrow because of His departure

II. **The Savior's Assertion (vv. 7–15)**
   A. The language analyzed
      1. "Nevertheless"—a strong, adversative "but"
      2. "I tell you the truth"—a formula for teaching truth
   B. It is "expedient"—better—for you if I go away
      1. If I go, the Comforter will come
      2. If I don't go, the Comforter won't come
   C. The merits of the case
      1. If I stay: I will be with you only, and only at certain times
      2. If I go: the Comforter will be in you, in all of you, and will be there at all times
   D. He will do tremendous things for you
      1. Things wrapped up in His name
         a. Comforter not best word choice
         b. Better—helper, encourager, strengthener
      2. He will be permanent and continuous (John 14:16–17)
      3. He will assist your ministry (vv. 8–11)
      4. He will teach you (vv. 12–15)
         a. Such things as all truth, things to come, and what is already available for you ("He shall receive of mine, and show it unto you")
         b. He will not speak from Himself but will glorify Christ by taking from Him and passing it on

(note statement is repeated twice for emphasis— vv. 14–15)

    E.   They were afraid of loneliness without Him, but He asserted that it would be better for them if they were left alone

III. The Believer's Assurance

    A   We may be alone at times and even feel lonely

    B.   We need never suffer from loneliness

        1.   Because we have the Holy Spirit within us

        2.   He not only indwells us but also does tremendous things for us

    C.   If we are suffering from loneliness

        1.   We may be failing to draw on the facts

           a.   Facts alone don't always seem to help

           b.   But they actually do, as emotions are the by-product of our thinking

        2.   We may be grieving the Holy Spirit

           a.   Did you ever notice how bitterness and loneliness often go together?

           b.   Grieving the Spirit will cut off the effect of His ministry to us

        3.   We may be focusing on self

           a.   Doing so causes us to dwell on how alone we are

           b.   We are not alone—we need to focus on others and get on with our lives

Conclusion:

It is unnecessary to suffer from loneliness. Why are you lonely? Are you failing to act upon truth? Are you grieving the Holy Spirit? Are you focused on self? Do you have the Holy Spirit within?

Jesus Asks, "What Is That to You?"
Matthew 19:16–20:16

Introduction:

Sometimes we have the same problem as the disciples—we get mixed up in things that aren't our business and get all concerned about them. Let's look at a story where this happened, but there is much background to be covered first.

I. **An Incident (19:16–22)**
    A. Details of a familiar story
       1. A man wants eternal life
       2. Christ tells him he can have it by obeying the law
       3. He says he has done so
       4. Christ shows him he has not by proposing he do something that would show he had actually done so
    B. He turns away, and Christ is sorrowful

II. **An Impression (19:23–26)**
    A. Christ's statement: It is very difficult for a rich man to be saved
    B. Disciples' response: We are beginning to think it is too hard for anyone to be saved
    C. Christ's response: It is too hard for man (as the rich tend to trust their riches), but nothing is too hard for God (He can get rich men to trust Him)

III. **Some Information (19:27–30)**
    A. Peter's question: We have left all to follow you. What will we get?
    B. Christ's answer:
       1. A place of authority in the future kingdom
       2. A reward in heaven
       3. But be careful as things are not always as they seem—some who pride themselves on being in the vanguard will barely make it; others who don't appear to make it at all may end up right in front

IV. **Some Illumination (20:1–16)**
    A. A man sends workers into field
       1. Man strikes an agreement with first group
       2. Just sends in other workers without an agreement
    B. Man gives orders at pay-off time
       1. Pay off the workers from last to first

       2. Doing so was bound to make first workers aware of the situation
- C. Consternation occurs
  1. First workers are unhappy and express it
  2. He gently rebukes them
     a. You got what you agreed to
     b. It is in my power to do as I wish

V. The Interpretation
- A. The main point—God is absolutely sovereign in what He bestows by way of reward
- B. Subpoints
  1. No one gets less than agreed to; some get more
  2. Things are not at all what they seem
  3. So long as you get what you have coming, what someone else gets is none of your concern but is up to God

VI. An Illustration (John 21:20–22)
- A. Christ predicts Peter's death
- B. Peter gets concerned about John's death
- C. Christ says: I am sovereign in that. I'll hand things out as I see fit. What is that to you?

VII. Some Implications: What is that to you?
- A. We get all concerned with God's dealings with others
  1. Some receive blessings
  2. Some receive problems
- B. We get all concerned with how we are dealt with in relation to others
- C. This even carries down to the realm of authority
  1. "I got more than he did"
  2. "I didn't get what he got"
- D. God ultimately controls what we get, so we need to worry less about others and accept what He sends into our lives

Conclusion:
Christian—don't be upset; just let God handle the score-keeping and rewarding. Unsaved person—it seems too hard to be saved, but with God all things are possible.

Jesus Tells Us How to Be Happy

John 15:1–7, 9–12

Introduction:

Happiness is a primary goal today. People seek it in all kinds of places and ways: alcohol, drugs, sex, rebellion. It is really found only in the Lord. He offers, in fact, something beyond happiness—joy! Finding it is easy to do and hard to understand—as this conversation shows.

I. **The Design (v. 11)**
   A. "These things have I spoken unto you" for two purposes
      1. That my joy might remain in you
      2. That your joy might be full
   B. God's purpose for us is that we be not only happy but that we go beyond happiness to joy
      1. Joy comes from Him as a gift (fruit of the Spirit)
      2. When we start with His joy, we can know fullness of joy

II. **The Details (vv. 1–7)**
   "These things have I spoken unto you." What things?
   A. He has spoken of two subjects
      1. Bearing fruit (vv. 1–6)—having a meaningful occupation
      2. Answered prayer (v. 7)—having needs met
   B. There is little else that one could ask for to have happiness and joy
      1. To be gainfully employed in meaningful, lasting tasks
      2. To have a source of supply for genuine needs
   C. These things are the source of joy
      1. They make life worth living
      2. They come from Him

III. **The Declaration (v. 9)**
   A. A designed sequence
      1. "I want you to have joy"
      2. Joy comes as you have meaningful occupation and as you have your needs met
      3. You'll know these two things as you abide in Me (vv. 4, 7)
   B. The condition for bearing fruit and having needs met is abiding in Him

      1. There's more confusion than you can believe over abiding
      2. Everyone wants to make it subjective
      3. Jesus summarizes it with "continue ye in my love"
  C. He then tells us how to do that
      1. Love always involves obedience
      2. Love also involves seeking to know Him better in the Word and prayer

IV. The Definition (v. 10)
  A. Abiding in Him is a simple matter of obedience
      1. There is nothing mystical about it
      2. It is just a matter of doing what He says
  B. Our source book is the Word
      1. The people to whom He was speaking had His direct teaching to go by
      2. We have in the Word everything He intended for us to have
  C. This actually includes all the subjective elements usually included
      1. Obviously covers reading Bible, prayer, meditation, etc.
      2. It goes beyond that and gets practical
  D. Summary
      1. God wants us to have joy and that joy comes from Him
      2. We can know it as we have spiritually meaningful occupation and our needs supplied
      3. We have those two factors as we abide in Him
      4. Abiding in Him is mainly a matter of obeying His Word

Conclusion:

Simply stated, joy is the result of obedience. Nothing ever seemed further from the truth, but nothing is more clear from the pages of the Word. If you are lacking joy, the problem may be one of performance. It could also be a matter of not having His presence in you in the first place. Then you need to begin with the question of salvation. There is no joy without that!

A Conversation About a New Commandment
John 13:34–35

Introduction:

When Jesus went back to heaven, He left a lot of good things behind for us. One of the best was the commandment, "Love one another." But there is so much misunderstanding on love. Someone has said, "While love attracts, fear repels. When love gives, lust grabs. What love builds, hatred destroys. With love, communication flourishes; with resentment, it withers. Love is the ultimate answer to all the problems of living" (Jay E. Adams, *The Christian Counselor's Manual* [Grand Rapids: Zondervan, 1973], 141). But we seem to know so very little about love, largely because we have been taught so much that is not correct. Let's see what we can learn from a conversation of Jesus.

I. **The Meaning of Love: "That ye also love one another"**
    A. Love always first involves action
        1. Shown by Christ's love for us (John 3:16)
        2. Love is first action and then feeling
        3. Love is giving of one's self (possessions, time, etc.) to meet the needs of another, and this involves awareness of needs
        4. Love takes action to meet those needs
    B. Love always has the best interest of the one loved at heart
        1. It always asks, "What is best for this person?"
        2. It never asks, "What will feel good to me?"

Genuine biblical love is always action directed toward another person that seeks to meet needs and promote his or her best interest. Such action results in the feelings of love.

II. **The Manner of Love: "As I have loved you, that ye also love one another"**

Note: He loved us as the Father loved Him (John 15:9).
    A. Unemotionally
        1. God and Christ did not base love on feeling (they didn't get all warm and wiggly when they got around us)
        2. Their love was based on the fact of our need and their desire to meet it
    B. Unconditionally (1 John 4:10)
        1. There was really little in us to love

17

2. He loved us before we ever loved Him
3. Much of our love is based on how people respond to us, but the real test is loving those who don't love you
C. Unendingly (John 13:1)
1. There was no end or limit to His love
2. We believe He loves no matter what
3. At what point does our love run out?
D. Unselfishly (1 John 3:16)
1. He loved them to the point of giving His life for them
2. For us this is more in willingness and attitude
3. Much of our focus is on whether people love us, but our love needs great unselfishness

III. **The Manifestation of Love: "By this shall all men know that ye are my disciples"**
A. This love is not natural
1. We already know it is not natural to us
2. This is not the common love of the world, which is generally based on the opposites of God's love
B. This love is revealing
1. When it is present, it is so different that it stands out
2. This is what believers are to be known for (not their stands, standards, or even beliefs)
C. This love is possible only through divine enactment
1. The only way you can know this kind of love is to know the One who commanded it
2. You can neither love nor be loved without His love

Conclusion:

How much do you know of, and practice, the love of which Christ speaks here? How does the world know you are a Christian? Do you need loving? If so, find someone and love him or her today.

The Conversations of Christ: Magnification

Luke 19:1–10

Introduction:

Jericho wasn't a nice place. It was a cursed city, and an area of difficult travel (e.g., the story of the Samaritan). It was a place filled with commerce and tax collectors. Jesus didn't have to go through there. He was on the way to the cross, and there were other ways to go. He had an individual in mind—a little fellow that He wanted to make much bigger.

I.   **The Story**
    A. Zacchaeus
        1. Chief among the publicans (tax collectors)
        2. He was rich
        3. So he was a rogue; that was the only way a tax collector could be rich in the Roman system
        4. He was curious about who or what was drawing the crowds, so he climbed a tree to see
    B. He was singled out by Christ to be His host while in the city
    C. He opened his home to Jesus
        1. The story here is only partially recorded; we are told nothing about what went on in the house
        2. We are told, however, about the murmuring outside
    D. Zacchaeus came out after the session with Christ and made public statements regarding his commitments
        1. I will give half of my goods to the poor
        2. I will restore to anyone from whom I have taken unjustly
    E. Christ comments approvingly on his statements

II. **What Is in View Here?**
    A. Some have seen Zacchaeus as announcing what he already was in the habit of doing (if so, there would have been no fuss over Jesus eating there)
    B. He is clearly telling what he intends to do from this point onward
    C. This is not hard to explain as he has just spent time with Jesus
    D. Jesus' comments made sense on this basis also

III. **What Do We Learn Here?**
    A. Change is inevitable

  1. A genuine encounter with Christ is sure to produce change
  2. This is in line with much New Testament teaching (1 Cor. 6:9–12; 2 Cor. 5:17; Eph. 5:1–8)
 B. Change is internal
  1. This is something more than the changes one makes as a result of "turning over a new leaf"
  2. This is the change that takes place in salvation
  3. It may not happen all at once
  4. It deals with the basic issues of life such as motives and beliefs
 C. Change is visible
  1. The change starts internally
  2. It always ends up visible
  3. There is a problem when the change is only visible (it is called hypocrisy)
  4. The changes we experience
   a. Always relate to key issues
   b. Show that key issues have been dealt with

Conclusion:

It isn't important if I believe you have changed; it is important that you have changed. If you have, I should believe you have been saved. Have you just dealt with outward things? If so, these changes won't last. Have you dealt with the real inside issues since you have been saved? God wants to change the person you are—real salvation will effect that—so that you can change the way you look, act, etc.

Practical Principles of Prosperity
Luke 12:13–34

Introduction:

There is a simple and practical way to master Scripture: just learn the principles of which it is full. The passage opens with some heavy teaching (vv. 1–12). Christ stopped for breath, and a bystander stepped in, seeking some type of official ruling to use against his brother and force a change. What started out as a conversation with a man about his inheritance turned into an expression of four principles that can guide us to prosperity in the sight of God.

I. **The Principle of Perspective (v. 15): A man's life consists not in the abundance of the things which he possesses**
    A. The background
        1. The man wanted Christ to side with him
        2. The man's raising the issue shows where he was coming from
        3. Jesus saw through his motive; he was interested in gain rather than justice—note the use of "things"
    B. "Things" are a threefold problem
        1. The temptation of "things"
        2. The temporality of "things"
            a. They don't last
            b. They don't satisfy
        3. The tyranny of "things" (if you are not careful, the things you own will end up owning you)
    C. Christ teaches that there is much more to life than "things" (to those who have them; to those who do not and wish they did)

II. **The Principle of Proportion (v. 21): He that lays up treasure for himself, and is not rich toward God (is a fool)**
    A. There is nothing wrong with man's success; one dimensional living is the problem
        1. The story deals with actual ownership of things
        2. The story shows the folly of living in time alone
    B. The story points at the need for balanced living when it comes to possessions (this is illustrated by the man with two stores)

C. Christ teaches that what we have on earth is only earthly, and on the importance of laying up treasures in eternity

III. The Principle of Priority (v. 31)
A. Christ gives further teaching
   1. Points out the folly of spending all our time and effort on human acquisition
   2. Says that we should not live in care-filled suspense regarding our needs
B. This is balanced teaching
   1. Material things should not occupy all our time and effort
   2. Paul's teaching fleshes out that of Christ; there is no contradiction
C. Christ is teaching that eternal concerns should be first in priority, because when they are, God will see to it that we get whatever else we need

IV. The Principle of Position (v. 34)
A. Christ stresses the importance of laying up treasure in heaven as well as on earth
   1. We do so through seeking the kingdom of God
   2. We also lay up treasure through things done in the name of the Lord Jesus
B. The teaching of verse 33 is relative
   1. It does not teach that it is wrong to have any savings, etc.
   2. It does teach that we would be wise to sell some of what we have and get treasure laid up in the right place
C. Christ is teaching that we place our hearts where our treasure is, so we need to get some treasure laid up in the Lord for our overall spiritual welfare

Conclusion:
God wants you more than He wants what you have. When He has you, then He can get what you have. There is no way an unsaved person can do what this calls for.

Jesus Said, "Follow Me"

Luke 9:23

Introduction:

This verse is part of a conversation with the disciples. It contains an interesting statement. The statement has been made difficult by the subjective interpretations often given. The real meaning, however, is very clear.

I. **The Demand for a Decision: "If any man will come after me"**
    A. Christ's invitations are always optional
        1. He confronts men
        2. He does not force men
    B. Man must decide whom he will follow
        1. Every man follows someone
            a. Self
            b. Satan
            c. The Savior
        2. Following is a matter of choice, and every man must decide if he will follow Christ

II. **The Requirement of Denial: "Let him deny himself"**
    A. Deny himself what?
        1. Various answers are given
        2. None seems fully adequate
    B. The real issue is best expressed: let him deny himself, period
        1. Set aside all personal means of securing salvation
        2. Own that someone else knows more than he
        3. Accept what that Person knows
    C. Clear implications: if a man wants to follow Christ
        1. He must stop doing it his own way
            a. Works
            b. Some philosophy
        2. He must do it Christ's way—there is no other—so every man must decide if he will follow Christ (if he will not, he will never find the way)

III. **The Demand Asserted: "And take up his cross daily"**
    A. Often misunderstood
        1. Some affliction, etc.
        2. Something in reference to Christ
    B. It refers to the price required for following Christ

C. The price is the result of identifying with Him
1. We can expect a small version of what He found
   a. Misunderstanding
   b. Ridicule
   c. Rejection
2. Notice Matthew 10:24
D. A man must decide if he will follow Christ, must do it His way, and must decide if the price is worth it (no "costless" discipleship in Bible)

IV. **The Discipleship Presented: "And follow me"**
A. An invitation presented
B. The invitation offers something
   1. Pattern provided (John 8:12)
   2. Partnership procured (John 14:21)
   3. Payment promised (1 Cor. 2:9)
C. The invitation makes an offer to balance what it costs

Conclusion:

Whom are you following? Christ? How? If you are not going His way, then you are not following. Are you paying a price? Will you follow Him?

What He Said About the Father's Business
Luke 2:41–50

Introduction:
We know little of His childhood (it is summarized in vv. 39–40). He emerges again at age twelve (the turning point year for Jewish youth). A trip to Jerusalem for the feast sets the stage. After they find Him, He asks two searching questions: (1) "How is it that ye sought me?" (2) "Wist ye not that I must be about my Father's business?" (v. 49). His Father's business was a dominant theme in His life. Let us look at His commitment to His Father's business as shown in this exchange.

I.   **Its Compulsion**
   A.   Repeated use of "I must" (Luke only: 9:22; 17:25; 22:37; 24:7)
   B.   He was driven by the shortness of His time (John 9:4)
      1.   He knew His timetable
      2.   It created great urgency for Him
   C.   He was completely committed to the purposes of His Father for His earthly life
      1.   He is not a vague and hazy character
      2.   He had more sense of direction and understanding of the future than anyone who has ever lived
   D.   He states early what later became His consuming compulsion: His Father's business

II. **Its Content: What was His Father's business?**
   A.   His ministry
      1.   He met physical needs
      2.   He dealt with social needs (properly understood)
      3.   He met spiritual needs
   B.   His statements
      1.   Preach the good news (Luke 4:43)
      2.   Die on the cross (Matt. 16:21)
      3.   Bring men to Himself (John 10:16)
   C.   Summary
      1.   His work was to meet the real needs of men
      2.   He came to seek and save the lost

III. **Its Conduct: How did He go about doing it?**
   A.   Total commitment
      1.   "Not my will but thine be done"
      2.   Nothing of Himself in His work

B. Wholehearted
   1. Nothing withheld
   2. He was completely consumed by the task at hand
C. Thoughtful
   1. He put His emphasis where it would do the most good
   2. He knew wise limitations for the disciples
D. He laid aside divine prerogatives and kept to priorities

IV. **Its Challenge: All this says something to us**
   A. Stated
      1. Christ had been sent to do His father's business
      2. Christ told us we are sent just as He was sent (John 17:18; 20:21)
   B. Explored
      1. What importance do we grant to the Father's business?
         a. It has been assigned to us by Christ
         b. Our prioritizing of it is crucial
      2. We have the same task assigned to us
         a. Meeting needs
         b. Meeting ultimate needs—bringing people to Christ
   C. Applied
      1. Christ's concern from childhood was His father's business
      2. Do you care about what Christ cared about?

Conclusion:
   Evangelism is at the center of the heart of God. It was the main purpose in Christ's coming, and the only reason God and Christ endured the cross. What part does evangelism, witnessing, soul-winning play in your life? You are not really about the Father's business until you are into it. Are you interested in what God is interested in?

The Conversation at Peter's Lowest Point

Mark 14:26–31, 66–72

Introduction:

A mark of the Bible's authenticity is the way it presents its own heroes. It shows men as they were and for what they were. There is no "cover up" on the pages of Scripture. One of the clearest portraits is that of Peter.

I. **His Lowest Point**
    A. The man—we can trace
        1. His background
        2. His character
        3. His call (he was already a disciple of John the Baptist when called to follow Christ)
    B. His leadership
        1. He was chosen first for a reason (he was a natural leader)
        2. He was articulate—so many things we would not know were it not for him
        3. He was a spokesman
            a. The two clearest statements of the disciples' faith come from him
            b. He probably (almost) always spoke for all
    C. His failure
        1. The basic issue in this passage was his threefold denial
            a. It was really a total failure
            b. He tried to deny he had ever even heard of Christ
            c. He tried to throw his accusers completely off the trail
        2. The factors that conditioned his denial
            a. He had a place of high privilege and leadership
            b. He had an adamant self-confidence of which he spoke repeatedly
            c. Christ's prediction: Peter went down, and he went down low—lower than most of us have ever gone; we would expect that his story would end at this point, but it doesn't

II. **His Highest Point**

Half of the book of Acts is concerned with Peter's leadership, and that story is tremendous.

A. His leadership in the early church
   1. He interpreted the miracle of Pentecost
   2. He performed the first apostolic miracle
   3. He fell before a servant girl; he stood before the Sanhedrin
   4. He presided at the Jerusalem council
B. His acceptance of positional change
   1. He dominates only first half of Acts
   2. He continues to lead but yields first place to Paul
   3. This may well be his highest point
C. His record of his own defection
   1. Mark paints the darkest picture of betrayal
   2. Peter was doubtlessly Mark's source
   3. He shows enormous power in detailing his own demise, so Peter rises from lowest depths to greatest heights, from cowardice to courage, from pettiness to power

III. **The Turning Point**
   A. His sorrow
      1. It was induced by the look of Christ (Luke 22:61)
      2. It was genuine (wept bitterly)
      3. It was productive (some of our problems stem from never really repenting)
   B. His encounter after the resurrection
      1. It was specific—to him alone
      2. It was significant—explained things
      3. It was determinative—established real conviction
   C. His restoration
      1. Just a quiet meeting
      2. Involved a careful reevaluation
      3. It was reassuring; note the threefold reaffirmation

Conclusion:

Peter stooped lower than most can conceive. Yet he rose to heights few have known. What caused that reversal was this experience with the Lord as it established who the Lord was and who Peter was in relationship to the Lord. No matter what you have or haven't been, God can work in you and use you.

Have You Stopped Beating Your Wife?
Mark 12:13–17

Introduction:
Some questions are almost impossible to answer. No matter what you say, you put your foot in your mouth. One good one is, "Do you still steal from your employer?" In this passage Christ is faced with one of these questions, and His reactions are most instructive.

I. **The Attitude of His Accusers**
    A. It is an attempt to trap
    B. It involves an unholy alliance (Pharisees-Herodians)
        1. Explain difference between the two groups
        2. Show how this would create dilemma
    C. They use unwholesome flattery
        1. Actually hypocrisy (v. 15)
        2. They spoke the truth without meaning to do so
        3. They were adding to a designed "set-up"
    D. They thought he could not escape the question
        1. There was a dual form to the question
        2. They tried to force a yes or no answer
    E. It is an unattractive revelation
        1. Shows much of Satan's method
            a. Strange alliance
            b. Measure of truth
            c. Subtlety of approach
        2. Reveals extent to which we must beware of Satan's wiles

II. **The Adequacy of His Answer**
    A. A startling request—asks for coin
        1. Not a direct answer
        2. Must have created a measure of surprise
    B. A careful avoidance
        1. He avoids two extremes
        2. Falling into a trap or giving no answer at all
    C. He unmasked their hypocrisy—He knew their hypocrisy and answered accordingly
    D. It provides pertinent teaching
        1. There is nothing wrong in careful answers (especially to loaded questions)

2. He is able to see through everything and everyone—you don't fool Him any more than they did

III. **Application of Authority: He not only answers, He answers authoritatively**
   A. Men have obligations in life
      1. There are things that are Caesar's and things that are God's
      2. He challenges their rebellion against obligation
   B. Men are responsible to fulfill life's obligations
      1. Render means to pay back
      2. Answers the "cop out" syndrome so common today
   C. Men need to know their obligations in life
      1. "To Caesar" the obligations are obvious—we are to obey rules and rulers
         a. Homage, obedience, and tribute
         b. With a conscience dependent on and enlightened by the limits of the Word
      2. "To God" the obligations are not always recognized
         a. Homage, obedience, and tribute
         b. He actually demands our whole selves
      3. Recognizing obligations hits key issues
         a. If you are unsaved, you are not rendering to God
         b. If you are not surrendered, you are not rendering to God either

Conclusion:

The coin with Caesar's picture goes to Caesar; the ruler gets that which bears his impress. You are made in the image and likeness of God and bear His image. The coin had to go back to Caesar or be misused. If you don't "pay back" to God, you are involved in a gross misuse, misappropriation. Have you stopped resisting God?

A Little Child Shall Lead Them
Mark 10:13–16

Introduction:
Everyone loves little children, that is, almost everyone. Sometimes, however, they get underfoot and create problems. The disciples had mixed emotions about them on at least one occasion, but that story teaches us much as we look at the three main actors in it.

I. The Disciples
They sought to keep the children from the Lord. This is conjecture, but did you ever wonder why?
  A. They wanted to spare Him the trouble (don't worry about the Lord, He can handle Himself)
  B. They felt like the children didn't need Him, certainly not like the other people there (there is a tendency sometimes to feel that children don't need the Lord)
  C. They felt the children couldn't understand what He could do (children often understand far more than we dream)
  D. They had forgotten the worth of the child

II. The Savior
  A. He was much displeased with the disciples
    1. This is not often said
    2. He must have been very indignant—saw them as missing a basic principle
  B. He was completely accepting
    1. This is typical of the Lord, who will accept anyone who comes to Him
    2. He wants no barriers placed in the way of coming to Him
  C. He used the children to teach a lesson—set them in the midst in a way to show that they reveal truth

III. The Children
They were passive actors, but they were an ideal object lesson for the disciples and for us.
  A. "For of such is the kingdom of God" is explained by verse 15: the kingdom of God is made up of people who are similar to a little child
  B. The similarities are not hard to identify

1. Children have great faith—it takes faith to enter the kingdom
2. Children are uncomplicated and can accept things for what they are—adults become so complicated that they can't accept the obvious
3. Children are not scarred by sin—many a person is unable to trust Christ because the scars of sin have hardened him
4. Children are able to do it someone else's way—adults have great trouble accepting someone's way that does not agree with theirs

C. Unless we take on the aspects of a child, we will not see the kingdom

Conclusion:

We should be seeking to bring the children to Christ. Woe to the one who blocks children from coming to Christ, and you can do this by your example as well as by your teaching. We can learn a great deal from the model of little children. Anyone who comes to Christ must come to Christ as a little child.

Lessons from a Loaf

Mark 8:1–21

Introduction:

We sometimes speak of people being at their "best" or their "worst." These are relative terms but helpful to our understanding. The passage before us shows some of each. Christ is functioning at His best. The disciples are at one of their low points.

I. **Christ at His Best (vv. 1–9)**
    A. Compassion
        1. He may have deliberately waited until they were without food to act
        2. He saw need and moved to meet it
    B. Ability
        1. He is always able to meet every need
        2. Further points
            a. Sometimes He does not choose to do so
            b. Sometimes He does so without being asked
            c. He promised to act when asked
    C. Operation
        1. He used something that they already had
            a. He does not normally work from nothing
            b. He does not eschew even the smallest amount
            c. He does require everything they have
        2. He uses disciples as He works miracles
        3. Beginning with something small, He accomplishes great things

II. **Disciples at Their Worst**
    A. This incident was triggered by His teaching (vv. 10–13)
        1. His encounter with the Pharisees
            a. They sought a sign (note: "from heaven") but were actually testing Him
            b. He refused their request and walked away from them
        2. He used it as teaching opportunity (v. 15)
    B. Their failure
        1. They assumed He was talking about failure to take bread
        2. They completely missed what He was trying to tell them
        3. This was an inexcusable failure
            a. It could be excused at beginning of chapter

33

b. There is no excuse now as they have witnessed two identical miracles

C. Their flaws are obvious from His questions
1. Insensitivity: thick-skinned hearts—"Have ye your hearts yet hardened"—and waterproofed minds
2. Failure to use the capacities they already had: "Having eyes, see ye not?" Failure to use powers results in their attrition
3. Absorption with material things
    a. Natural area of concern
    b. They were so absorbed they missed Him
    c. Christ has always been obstructed by materialism
4. Failure to remember

III. **The Tension Between Them**
A. Christ's rebuke
1. Rare display of strong emotion
2. His shows a deep concern

B. Showed three reactions
1. Astonishment
    a. He was learning (as human) firsthand the depth of human stupidity
    b. He must wonder at our unbelief
2. Pain
    a. Failure of belief upset Him
    b. Sometimes believers hurt the Lord the most
3. Indignation
    a. Wrath and gentleness combined in Him
    b. He had no desire to hurt, but deeply felt emotions

C. Closed with corrective reproof (vv. 19–21)

Conclusion:

Christ rebuked His disciples because they had forgotten. They had lost track of what He had done. They had allowed other things to crowd in. We are also prone to quickly forget lessons, blessings, and provisions. The disciples missed the whole point because of their preoccupation with other things.

A Conversation with Peter About Worth
Matthew 19:27–30

Introduction:
   You are involved in a fairly demanding task, and right in the middle of it you wonder if it is really worth it. You are doing a project, and right in the middle of it you wonder if what you are doing is enough. Most of us are plagued by the uncertainties of insecurity—especially as it pertains to spiritual things—and so were the disciples in this story.

I. **The Question That Prompted the Discourse (v. 27)**
   A. The one who asked it—Peter
      1. The most outspoken and also the unofficial spokesman for the group
      2. Exactly the one whom we would expect
   B. The background of it
      1. They had just heard Christ telling the rich young man that he must sell all that he has in order to be worthy of eternal life
      2. This no doubt raised some feelings within the disciples as they had left everything they had and followed Him
   C. The question itself
      1. Related to Christ's answer to the rich young man
         a. Peter may have been trying to be sure of the kingdom—had they passed the test the young man failed?
         b. Christ's answer shows, however, that there was more involved
      2. The question actually covers two areas
         a. Have we done enough to make it?
         b. Is it really worth all we have left behind?
      3. The question still gets asked today in various forms
         a. What is enough to satisfy the Lord?
         b. Is Christianity worth all that I might have to give up?
         c. Is discipleship really worth it?

II. **The Answer That Settled the Issue (vv. 28–29)**
   A. A specific word to the disciples (v. 28)
      1. He gives them a particular promise of a future position, a future function, and a future date

        2. He answered their question of whether or not they
           had done enough
           a. He shows them what He had in store for them
           b. He goes back to the rich man: they hadn't
              learned the lesson—they had already shown
              sufficient love by leaving and following
    B. A general promise to all disciples
        1. It is made to those who have left position,
           possessions, and relations
        2. It is made to those who have done so for the right
           reasons—for my sake and the gospel's—not for
           mere religion, etc.
        3. It contains some wonderful truths
           a. A reward in time: a hundredfold—a vast
              proportion (note that it does not necessarily
              have to be in exact kind)
           b. A reward in eternity

Peter asked, "Have we done enough?" Christ said, "Yes."
Peter asked, "Is it worth it?" Christ said, "Yes," in both time and
eternity.

III. The Warning That Emphasized the Lesson (v. 30)
    A. A common statement that Christ used in at least one
       other place
        1. It may have been a proverbial expression
        2. It had several possible meanings
    B. A difficult usage
        1. It isn't easy to decide why it was used in this place
        2. There are several possibilities
    C. A suggested explanation
        1. Christ was stressing the standard by which things
           are actually measured: He does not measure as we
           do, as His measure is the only just and accurate one
        2. Christ was stressing the inwardness of truly
           spiritual things in contrast to the outwardness so
           common
    D. Some important applications
        1. You may question if it is enough: that is an internal
           matter between you and the Lord, but you must be
           sure of it or you could be one of the first who turns
           up last
        2. You may ask whether or not it is worth it. The real
           question may be do you have anything to give
           up that's worth anything, or have you given up
           anything worthwhile?

Conclusion:

Peter had two questions: (1) Have we done enough? (2) Is it worth it? Men ask the same questions today. Let's face facts; only you can know whether or not it is enough by knowing whether or not you love Him enough to accept Him. There are some things to give up for Christ, but they are insignificant in contrast to what we get. Only you and God know what you have and haven't given.

The Conversation with Satan at the Temptation
Matthew 4:1–11

Introduction:
I once saw a man who was not tempted. When I saw him, he had been dead for three days. No living man has ever been free of temptation—not even the Lord Jesus.

I. **The Background of His Temptation**
   A. The events leading up to it
      1. Following his ministry's introduction at His baptism
      2. The sequence is immediate
   B. Was this the only time Christ was tempted?
      1. It wasn't—during the whole forty days and afterward (see Luke), later by Peter, and in the garden
      2. This conditions our treatment of Hebrews 4:15
   C. Why did Christ face this?
      1. Because He had to face and settle some issues once and for all before facing them repeatedly
      2. Because it provided an opportunity to demonstrate His determination to follow the Father's will for Him
      3. Because it prepared Him for the pressures He would experience in the world of sin and among the false-hoping Jews

II. **The Temptation Itself**
   A. First encounter
      1. Form: after forty-day fast, and a great temptation to a hungry man , the appeal was to use His powers to take care of His hunger
      2. Thrust: an appeal to meet needs in His own way rather than accepting hunger that was in the will of God
      3. Answer: physical welfare is not of primary importance; the proper way to meet the need of Himself and the world was God's way
   B. Second encounter
      1. Form: a misquotation of Scripture—Cast thyself down to prove God
      2. Thrust: really an appeal to demonstrate lack of trust

3. Answer: it is not right to try the Lord (confident faith eliminates need for putting God to the test)
C. Third encounter
   1. Form: vision of all kingdoms of the world, and Satan had the power to render them (Luke 4:6)
   2. Thrust: attempt to get Christ to achieve something outside the will of God; it would be strongly appealing because Christ knew what was coming
   3. Answer: only God should be worshipped; the kingdoms will be His at the proper time and in the proper way

III. The Lessons to Be Learned
A. The main point: the whole thrust of Satan was to get Him to operate outside the will of God, and this is the basis of all temptation
B. There is no sin in being tempted—yielding, not temptation, is sin
C. Temptation comes in many forms—some obvious, some much more subtle, all appealing
D. Satan is extraordinary in his approaches—came right into the temple (in the midst of our religious life); he will even misquote Scripture (most heresies, sects, are based upon this fact)
E. Temptations must be met with the Word and not just by quoting it; use the Word at points where we are in accord with it in our lives
F. Temptations endured lead to greater spiritual greatness; the greatness of the untried man is never really proven
G. If Christ could triumph, so can we; He was subject to temptation as representative man (if we can live because of His death, we can triumph because of His triumph)

Conclusion:
Troubled soul, are you under temptation? Remember that there is no sin in being tempted as conformity to the will of God is being tested. The Word of God is the "weapon of choice" in facing temptation. He triumphed and so can you.

Let's Talk About Fishing
Matthew 4:17–22

Introduction:

Most men love to fish. Some don't even care if they catch any fish—they just like to go fishing. But did you ever consider that the image you have of fishing may be wrong? You've always imagined "fishers of men" to be a certain way, and it isn't. Most of us have a wrong concept about this metaphor. It isn't sport fishing; it is commercial fishing. But they're the same, aren't they? Not on your life!

I. **Commercial Fishing Is Serious Business**
   A. It is not necessarily fun (like any job)
   B. It is hard, demanding, exhausting work
      1. Whether or not one likes to do it is immaterial
      2. When He said "fishers of men," He meant commercial fishermen, who view it as serious business

II. **Commercial Fishing Is Done All the Time**
   A. Sport fishing is a "sometime" thing
   B. Commercial fishing is a daily affair—even in very bad weather
      1. When He said "fishers of men," the disciples understood commercial fishing
      2. Commercial fishing is done all the time

III. **Commercial Fishermen Know They Won't Always Catch Fish but Go Anyway**
   A. Note the story in John 21, in which they fished all night
   B. It's one thing to go when it's fun; it's quite another to go when you know that at times you'll catch nothing, but it must be done anyway
   C. When He said "fishers of men," this is what they understood Him to mean

IV. **Commercial Fishermen Try to Catch All They Can**
   A. They don't fool around—the name of the game is catching fish, not just going fishing
   B. They use nets rather than hooks
   C. They try to gather up all they can—they don't just fool around

V. Commercial Fishermen Keep All They Can
    A. They know that all won't be keepers
    B. They try to keep and use all they can
        1. They are after tonnage not trophies
        2. They have some unique usage—some "scallops" are actually monkfish
    C. They don't throw them back or let them slip away

Conclusion:

He still gives the invitation to those who follow Him. He will make them fishers of men, but it is commercial fishing He has in mind. Commercial fishing is a serious business. It is pursued all the time. It is done even when there are no fish caught. It goes after every possible fish. And it seeks to keep all that is caught. Are you a fisher of men in the sense He intended?

A Chat with Some Disciples About Service

Matthew 8:18–22; Luke 9:57–62

Introduction:
"And I promised Him that I surely would serve Him until I die"—did you really? You know there's more to service than meets the eye. Some of the conversations of Christ prove it.

I. **With a Certain Scribe**
    A. The background
        1. We accept Matthew's chronology as the accurate one
        2. Christ is about to withdraw from His public ministry
        3. He has just completed His miracles
    B. The incident
        1. Scribe speaks: "Master, I will follow thee withersoever . . ."
        2. Christ answers: The Son of Man doesn't even have what the animals have—a permanent resting place
        3. His answer examines the man
            a. Do you really know what you are saying?
            b. Do you really wish to follow?
    C. The implications
        1. Christ makes no attempt to hide the price of following
        2. His poverty was part of His humiliation
        3. The man who comes after Him will have to adopt an attitude of detachment, realize no permanent moorings here, and be willing to face the existence of a nomad

II. **With an Unnamed Disciple**
    A. The background
        1. The man was a disciple
        2. It may have been Thomas
    B. The incident
        1. Christ issues a call to service; the disciple had already been called (Luke 9:59)
        2. The man responds, "Suffer me first to go and bury my father"—either his father had just died or he wants to stay until his father does die
        3. The examining answer, Jesus repeats initial invitation: "Let the dead bury their dead: but go thou and preach" (Luke 9:60)

C. The implications
1. Christ's call to service is superior to the highest of earth's obligations
2. If it was a matter of waiting for father's death
   a. No human ties should keep us back
   b. He might have missed the whole ministry of Christ (we must always be careful of God's timing)
3. If it was a matter of his father having already died
   a. It shows that there are times when the call of Christ rises above every human obligation
   b. It sharpens the focus of priorities in our relationships
4. Christ exemplified this in His relationship to Mary; He showed love and concern, but there are three places where He sets her aside

III. With an Unidentified Man (Luke 9:61–62)
A. The background
1. Not recorded in Matthew; little information is given in Luke
2. We don't know if he was a disciple or not
3. Actually, it may have been Matthew
B. The incident
1. The call of Christ—not recorded but implied by the story's following the other two
2. The man responds—he is willing to follow, but he wants some time first
3. The examining answer
   a. Answer reveals man's problem
   b. He was evidently tied to the past and inclined to waver
C. The implications
1. Christ's call demands immediate response
2. The ties of the past must be broken in order to adequately serve Him
3. There is no place in His service for those who waver

Conclusion:
Three men face service: (1) the impulsive; (2) the one facing conflicting duties; (3) the one with a divided mind. The demands are put forth for service: placed above all material ties and placed above all half-heartedness. A man must count the cost before following Christ. Having done so, though, it's all the way!

Talking with the Pharisees and John's Disciples About Eating

Matthew 9:9–17; Mark 2:13–22; Luke 5:27–39

Introduction:
The record of the Gospels is the record of the Master among men. He was always moving among men and always talking with them. Three encounters are especially interesting for what they teach.

I. **His Encounter with Levi (Matthew)**
    A. This adds one more outcast to those among whom He moved
        1. Matthew was a publican—tax collector
        2. He was hated because of the way the system operated
    B. There is a call and a response
        1. "Follow me"
        2. The response is immediate (he probably left immediately)
        3. This took some faith as he was abandoning his profession
    C. There is important teaching here
        1. Everyone saw a hated tax collector
        2. Christ saw the man—what he really was and could be

II. **His Encounter with the Pharisees**
    A. The background of the incident
        1. Luke tells us Matthew gave Him a feast
        2. He invited his friends—an unsavory bunch but probably all he knew
    B. Objections were raised
        1. The objections were brought to the disciples
        2. Objections had to do with eating with "defiled" people
        3. Actually, the Pharisees had some grounds for complaint
    C. Adequate answers are given
        1. Jesus answers for the disciples
        2. His answer takes three forms but makes no attempt to defend
            a. I am a physician—the sick need me, not the well

b. You misunderstand God; He wants hearts not ritual

c. A statement of purpose

D. Lessons are taught

1. Jesus went where the need was—we wait for the need to come to us

2. There is no contamination in contact so long as we are on a mission and go with Him

3. There are always those who will criticize a ministry that mixes with sinners

III. **His Encounter with the Disciples of John**

A. A question asked

1. We practice religious asceticism; you do not. Why is it that you don't?

2. They were actually questioning whether He truly understood the seriousness of life and spiritual life

B. An answer given

1. He uses illustration of marriage

2. He speaks of a "taking away"—a word for forcible removal, an intimation of His impending death

3. Christ defends the right of His people to be merry

C. Further teaching is given

1. Two illustrations are used

2. Both provide answers to His detractors

a. They accused Him of failing to understand the seriousness of religion

b. He showed them that there were things they didn't understand

3. The nature of the answer

a. You can't take this new thing I have brought and merge it into the old—it won't work

b. You can't take this new thing I have brought and pour it into the confines of the old

Conclusion:

Jesus came to bring healing to sinners, so He moved among them. As He did He saw men for what they really were and could become, and He brought them something new and vital. Christ still moves among men, seeing them for what they are and still offers them something new. But as then, when the Pharisees and John's disciples rejected what He had to offer, so today men reject Him even as He moves among them.

He Speaks with the Disciples About the Harvest
Matthew 9:35–10:42

Introduction:
The key note in the operation of Christ was to move among men—always, ever, continually. He is still at it in verse 35—moving among men. As He does, we catch something of His heart.

I. **Jesus' Reaction to the Multitudes**
   A. "When he saw the multitudes"
      1. Great crowds thronged Him
      2. The multitudes included people of all types, etc.
      3. He saw them as individuals
   B. "He was moved with compassion on them"
      1. Moved with compassion: the old idea was that the intestines were the seat of emotions; He was so deeply moved it affected Him physically
      2. The compassion of Christ
         a. It was the great compelling force in redemption, it was love defined: feeling with, suffering pain with, comradeship in sorrow
         b. It fully expressed itself on the cross

II. **Jesus' Recognition of the Multitudes**
   A. Three things describe them
      1. "Were faint"— is an emasculated translation—more like harassed, vexed
      2. "Scattered abroad"—from throw, toss, exposed
      3. "Sheep having no shepherd"—wandering, adrift, cut loose
   B. This is really an apt description of the masses
      1. Men are harassed, vexed in spite of their contrary protestations
      2. Men are beaten and thrown about in spite of their feelings of self-direction
      3. Men are as dumb animals without leadership
   C. Jesus recognized some things we need to recognize
      1. The awful condition of lost men
      2. The desperate need of lost men
      3. The lost sheep aspect of lost men

III. **Jesus' Response to the Multitudes**
   A. An evaluation of the enormity of their need; He saw the need and realized their inability to meet it

B. He presents a picture
    1. A great harvest—notice that the harvest is great, not just the harvest field
    2. A scarcity of laborers—workers
C. He prompts a prayer
    1. "Pray ye therefore the Lord of the harvest"—note that He is Lord of the harvest and don't focus too much on methods
    2. "Pray . . . that he will send forth laborers"—they are asked to pray first (where all responsive concern begins)
    3. It is His harvest
D. He provides personnel (10:1–4)
    1. He chose the very ones who had been praying as they were the ones prepared
    2. He gives them power, and at this point the name switch takes place—from disciple to apostle
E. He pronounces the particulars—three ministry timeframes
    1. Immediate ministry (10:5–15) up to Calvary
    2. Near future (10:16–23) from cross to destruction of Jerusalem 70 A.D.
    3. Distant future (10:24–42) from destruction of Jerusalem to second advent

Jesus' response to the multitude is to burden men with their need, send those men to meet it, and provide them with what they need to do the job

Conclusion:

Multitudes are still unreached. Jesus still seeks to reach them through other men. Before we are ever going to reach them, though, we must see their awful plight and share Christ's great compassion for them. Pray and go.

A Conversation About Moving Mountains
Matthew 17:14–21

Introduction:
I've known of several people who died apparently because they had too much faith— they trusted in a "healer" or something similar. But can you really have too much faith? Not really, but you can have the wrong kind of faith or faith in the wrong thing. How about faith to move mountains, for instance? Or to transplant sycamore trees?

I. **Faith Statements**
   A. The grain of mustard seed is exceedingly small
   B. The moving of mountains
      1. We are twice told that mountains can be moved (Matt. 17:14–21; Mark 11:22–26)
      2. Once we are told that we can transplant sycamore trees (and have them take root in the sea)
   C. The declaration involved—"ye shall say"

II. **Faith Meanings**
   Can you actually move mountains or transplant sycamores?
   A. Note the contexts
      1. Matthew 17—after the disciples' inability to cast out demons
      2. Mark 11—after the withering of fig tree
      3. Luke 17—after the teaching on forgiveness
   B. Obviously each situation deals with something very difficult
      1. "Mountain" and "sycamore tree" appear to be figurative for great difficulty
      2. Each could actually have reference to the concept of the impossible

III. **Faith Implications**
   Jesus does teach that you can do the impossible through faith—even a little bit of faith.
   A. If it really is impossible
      1. No real impossibility in mountain moving now
      2. But belief in the "economy of the miraculous" makes it unlikely
   B. If it is necessary
      1. There is no real necessity to transplant a sycamore (God is not interested in "showy" miracles)

2. God will not normally provide a miracle just for the sake of the miracle
C. If it glorifies God
   1. In each biblical instance, there was glory brought to God by the miracle
   2. God is not interested in glorifying anyone but His Son and Himself, so it must be in the will of God
D. We absolutely must consider the glory of God
   1. This is not a means of "cop-out" or nonanswer
   2. He has a plan, and He knows absolutely what is best

IV. **Faith Applications**
   A. Don't underrate the power of God
      1. He can—and does—do the impossible
      2. Don't give up on anything
   B. Don't forget the qualifications
      1. He rarely does what can be done another way
      2. He likely won't do what doesn't need to be done
      3. He is most interested in what glorifies Him
      4. He will exert His will no matter what; we might as well settle this issue at the start
   C. Don't forget the rest of the stories
      1. The need for intensity to accomplish (Matthew)
      2. The importance of forgiveness (Mark)
      3. The need of faith to do the difficult, routine things (Luke)

Conclusion:

You can move mountains and transplant sycamore trees. But it has to be for the right reasons and under the proper conditions. Has something in your life not moved? Consider,

- Is it impossible?
- Is it necessary?
- Is it to glorify God?
- Is it in His will?

And are you meeting the qualifications?

Jesus Talks About Forgiveness

Matthew 18:21–35

Introduction:
Forgiveness lies right at the heart of God. Men tend to struggle with either accepting or granting forgiveness. Jesus was very clear on His position concerning it.

I. **The Inquiry (vv. 21–22)**
    A. Peter's question
        1. No doubt prompted by Christ in verse 15
        2. Aren't there limits to this forgiveness business?
        3. He actually suggests a generous limit for a Jew
    B. Christ's answer
        1. He rejects the limits Peter sets
        2. He gives a vast number—without limit
        3. In essence He says that there is no limit to forgiveness

II. **The Illustration (vv. 23–34)**
    A. A king and his servant
        1. Details
            a. The servant owed the king a great amount
            b. King orders "liquidation of assets," and the servant pleads for mercy
            c. The king goes beyond his request
        2. Design—it shows the relationship between a sinner and his God
            a. The enormity of debt (all sins are big sins) and the right of the king to seek payment
            b. The penalty to be exacted
            c. The poverty of the servant and his plea for mercy
            d. The fullness of pardon granted
    B. The servant and his fellow servant
        1. Details
            a. The smallness of the debt
            b. The violence of the action
            c. The demand
            d. The plea for mercy—identical to his own
            e. The self-defeating action
        2. Describes a forgiven sinner who refuses to forgive
            a. He has been forgiven large and is unwilling to forgive small

   b. Human passion involved

   c. He refuses identical plea to his own and defeats himself

  C. The king and his judgment

   1. Details

    a. Report comes to him

    b. Rebuke comes from him, and he reminds of the forgiveness granted and remonstrates for the lack of forgiveness shown

    c. The result—loss of the forgiveness granted

   2. Describes the reaction of God to our failure to forgive (Matt. 6:14–15)

III. The Implication

  A. Stated (v. 34)

   1. God will do the same to you that you do to others, that is, remove your forgiveness

   2. Forgiveness must be from the heart

  B. Explored

   1. Failure to forgive is illogical

   2. Failure to forgive will result in failing to be forgiven

   3. Failure to forgive will result in unanswered prayer (Matt. 11:25–26)

   4. Failure to forgive results in harm to the one who fails to forgive rather than to the one not forgiven

   5. Failure to forgive has as its alternative the simple fact of bitterness

Conclusion:

Forgiveness must be sought to be granted. There must be a confession of having done wrong before it can be granted, otherwise all you have is some form of an apology. Forgiveness must be registered in the heart whether or not it is sought. Who have you failed to forgive? Have you ever sought God's forgiveness? He is the only one who could make you able to forgive in the sense given in this passage.

Jesus Talks About Caesar's and God's

Matthew 22:15–22

Introduction:

Did you ever get between a rock and a hard place? In the story before us, Christ was put there by His enemies. The manner in which He handled it and the truth He taught while He was handling it are both most instructive.

I. **The Plot**
   A. He has been using parables that the Pharisees sense describe them
   B. They deliberately seek to entangle Him in His talk
      1. They hope to put Him on the spot by a trap
      2. They send those who might not be recognized

II. **The Presentation**
   A. Strange bedfellows come
      1. These people hated each other
      2. Men often get together for the strangest reasons
   B. They come with flattery
      1. "Master"—one with teaching authority—"we know that thou art true"
      2. You "teachest the way of God in truth"
      3. "Neither carest thou for any man"—you are not easily intimidated
      4. "Thou regardest not the person of men"—you are not threatened by Roman authority
   C. All they said was true; it was said for the wrong reasons in this situation

III. **The Probe**
   A. There is much more here than meets the eye
   B. The question: "Is it lawful to give tribute unto Caesar, or not?" (Is it correct in the sight of God?)
   C. It was clearly designed to create a "rock and hard place" situation
      1. "Yes" shows Him unworthy to represent God and loses the people
      2. "No" shows Him as an insurrectionist to be reported to Rome

IV. **The Perception**
   A. He saw through what they were doing

       1. They didn't want an answer—they had a trap
       2. Many of our questions seek no answers; they are diversionary at best
  B. He put His finger on it: "Why tempt ye me?"
  C. He called them hypocrites
       1. They didn't mean what they had said to Him
       2. Neither group lived by what it claimed (Pharisees paid tribute; Herodians tried to get out of it)

V. The Position

  A. He asked for the coin of tribute
       1. Taxes were paid in Roman coins so they brought Him one
       2. He asks, "Whose is this image and superscription?"
  B. He then states the principle
       1. Give to Caesar what belongs to Caesar
       2. Give to God what belongs to God
  C. Three truths arise out of this
       1. There is a difference between God and Caesar
       2. Both have rightful claims (rules out idea that we don't have to pay taxes)
       3. We are obligated to give each his rightful due

VI. The Power

  A. Christ has answered the question: He simply says that what is, is; and there is nothing that can be done about it but obey
  B. His words have impact on them
       1. They marveled
       2. They left Him—stopped setting traps

VII. The Principle

  A. We are condemned by His answer
       1. We do very well with what belongs to Caesar
       2. We do not do well with what belongs to God
  B. There are many illustrations of our failure
       1. We pay taxes but withhold the tithe
       2. We obey when the officer is around but forget "thou God sees me"
       3. We do what governmental authority says and ignore the authorities God has placed over us
  C. Three passages tell us what God does require of us (Deut. 10:12; Mic. 6:8; Rom. 12:1–2)

Conclusion:

Are you a law-abiding citizen who gives Caesar his due? How do you fare in regard to what God requires? Do you give? Do you obey? Do you live as He demands? Is it not time to be sure you render to God His due just as you render to Caesar his due?

The Conversation with Nicodemus About Eternal Life

John 3:1–19

Introduction:

Few passages of Scripture are more familiar than this one. Few incidents teach a crucial truth more clearly. Few sermons need to be preached more than this one.

I. **Consider Nicodemus**
    A. He was credentialed: he had it all so far as Jewry was concerned
    B. He was cautious: notice that he "came . . . by night"
    C. He was curious: the things of God were stirring in his heart
    D. He was somewhat condescending: his approach is not quite as respectful as it appears
    E. He was confronted: he came to question; he was questioned instead
    F. He was confused: both at the start and particularly after Christ's statements to him
    G. He was corrected: he went away knowing the full truth
    H. He was challenged: basic question—what are you going to do with all this?

II. **The Main Movements of the Conversation**
    A. John 3:1–8: the introductory question that is answered by getting to the real question that he wanted answered
    B. John 3:9–12: the incredulous response and the mild remonstrance concerning his inexcusable ignorance
    C. John 3:13–17: the crux of the matter clearly stated in verses 16–17
    D. John 3:18–21: the additional details and explanation

III. **Truths That Jump Off the Page**
    A. The miraculous in the ministry of Christ is peripheral
    B. The new birth is central
    C. There is no other way to heaven other than through the new birth
    D. The Spirit cannot be seen, but His effects are obvious
    E. God is love, and this means that He will always act in love
    F. The giving of God's Son involved two aspects

      1.   Deliverance from sin and death
      2.   The granting of eternal life
G.   "Eternal life" has more to do with quality of life than with its duration
H.   Eternal life and eternal condemnation begin here and now
I.   Eternal life is just that—eternal in both quality and duration
J.   The decision that determines which of these two a man will have is made by the man himself
K.   The decision for eternity is made in time

Conclusion:

It is a most familiar passage. It really is a rather simple story. It cuts right to the very heart of why Jesus came. It presents men with an inescapable challenge.

Some Conversations with the Disciples About True Greatness

Matthew 18:3–4; 20:20–28; Mark 9:33–37; 10:35–45;
Luke 9:46–48; 22:24–30

Introduction:
Our society is greatly concerned about issues of "greatness." We revere our "heroes" even when they are unworthy. We strive for the "top" even when it costs more than it pays. This phenomenon is not new. Jesus had to face it and its implications during His earthly ministry.

I.   **It's a Really Big Deal!**
   A. There were so many misconceptions about the Messiah that Jesus had to deal with an enormous amount of cultural "baggage"
   B. Many misunderstandings had to do with "kingdom" issues (the Jews, generally speaking, looked for the reestablishment of the political kingdom)
   C. The disciples were sufficiently human that they were deeply concerned with such matters as "pecking order"
   D. How's this for a Jewish mother? Even the mother of two disciples got into the mix (Matt. 20:20–21)

II. **It's No Big Deal at All!**
   A. Jesus pointed out to the disciples that they suffered from cultural confusion in that they were trying to do it the Gentile way (Matt. 20:25)
   B. Jesus explained to the intrusive mother that His kingdom was something entirely different and, thus, greatness in it would be different as well (Matt. 20:22–23)
   C. Jesus promised that the kingdom would be future and that there would be both rewards and future equality for His followers (Luke 22:28–30)

III. **When the Converted Need Conversion**
   A. He says, "Whosoever therefore shall humble himself as this little child, the same is greatest in the kingdom of heaven" (Matt. 18:4), indicating that true greatness involved great simplicity rather than complexity
   B. Does Jesus suggest a second conversion (Matt. 18:3)? It appears He is speaking about a necessary change

of mind and approach (in other words, they had it all backward and needed to get it straight)

IV. **A New and Better Way**
    A. Leadership qualifications (Luke 22:27)
        1. He cites His own example as normative
        2. This is one of the passages that establishes the concept of "servant leadership"
    B. Paul expounds further on the example of Christ
        1. He went down to get up (Phil. 2:1–11)
        2. "Wherefore" shows that His exaltation was related to His humiliation
    C. The same statement is repeated (Matt. 19:30; Mark 10:31; Luke 13:30); it is as if He is asking, "Did you get it?"

V. **How Come John Never Mentions All This?**
    A. Oh, but he does (John 13:1–20)
        1. This may be the ultimate explanation of the meaning of true greatness
        2. There are aspects here that almost defy comprehension (such as the fact that He washed the feet of Judas)
    B. Actually, this is a recurring theme in the entire New Testament
        1. Paul identifies his "claim to fame" as something far different from what his world would have recognized
        2. James never used his relationship to Jesus as a "pry bar" to greatness

VI. **The One Who "Slices to the Bone"**
    A. Jesus comprehended the normal approach to greatness in His time
    B. He absolutely reversed it to the point that His definition is a new one

Conclusion:

Seems everyone wants to get ahead today and achieve greatness. "Upward mobility" is often built on the bodies of those used in the quest. There is a "price of fame," and many seem willing to pay it. Jesus comes with a completely new concept—servant leadership. He shows that the pathway up is first a pathway down into humility. He provides the perfect example. Why is it that so many of us seem to be unaware of His approach—at least in our practice?

Talking with the Pharisees About Hand Washing
Matthew 15:1–20

Introduction:
The Pharisees really had a lot of hang-ups, and most of them had to do with the ways in which religious acts were done. They had a rule for just about everything, and most of those rules had little or nothing to do with anything. For some reason men appear to be attracted to rules (probably because they make life easier and less complex). Although mindful of the rules laid down by His Father (the Ten Commandments), Jesus really had little time for rules. This exchange is most instructive.

I. **The Pharisees Said, "Your Boys Don't Play by the Rules"**
    A. The specifics: they don't do the ceremonial hand-washing before they eat
    B. The source: these rules came from reference to Scripture, but they were crafted and embellished by tradition

II. **Jesus Said, "You Boys Don't Even Know the Rules"**
    A. A condemnation: "You transgress the commandments of God by your tradition"
    B. A citation: He points out the clever way that had been devised to get out of caring for parents

III. **They Were Guilty of Hardcore Hypocrisy**
    A. Confusion: You think you have it all straight, but it really is completely backward
    B. Clarification: He uses Scripture to point out their situation (Isa. 29:13)

IV. **So the Question Is Raised, "Is It Inside Out or Outside In?"**
    A. A simple statement: not what goes into the mouth but what comes out of the mouth defiles the man (v. 11)
    B. A specific explanation: things that go into the mouth pass on through the body; things that are in the man make their way out of the mouth (vv. 16–20)
    C. A deliberate challenge: Pharisees upset? He seems to say, "So what?"

V. **He Provides a "Fall Catalog" of Sins!**
    A. Evil thoughts: all thinking out of accord with genuine truth

B. Murders: the malice that leads to murder
C. Adulteries and fornications: all forms of moral impurity
D. Thefts: taking away the goods of others without their knowledge or consent
E. False witness: concealing truth or giving false information
F. Blasphemies: speaking evil of, to injure by words
G. Covetousness: wanting what someone else has, and wanting it badly enough to take it
H. Wickedness: a desire to injure others
I. Deceit: the desire to benefit one's self by doing injustice to others
J. Lasciviousness: unbridled sexual sins
K. An evil eye: looking for opportunities to do evil to or to hurt others
L. Pride: an improper estimate of one's own importance
M. Foolishness: choosing bad ends and/or bad means of achieving them

VI. **And So, It's All a Matter of Focus**
   A. Internal versus external
   B. Spirit versus flesh
   C. Big versus little
   D. An important clarification: the "catalog items" don't keep us from salvation or cause us to lose salvation; they just indicate the lack of salvation (or they demonstrate the absence of a right heart)

Conclusion:
There seems to be so much of the Pharisee in most modern Christianity. There is so much emphasis on external factors such as how we dress or look, where we go, what we do or don't do, and the like. Although there is surely some importance to these external issues, they often obliterate the real spiritual issues. Biblical Christianity is not outside in, but is inside out.

Talking to Simon About the "Weeping Woman"
Luke 7:36–50

Introduction:
Someone has said, "Don't talk about being Christlike unless you know some alcoholics, prostitutes, and I.R.S. agents." That's probably good advice as these kinds of people played a prominent place in the life of the Lord. (He even was around a lot of Pharisees.) Contact with Christ can bring out the best in the worst of us.

I. **A Lukewarm Invitation**
    A. Simon, the Pharisee, invites Jesus to dinner
    B. Subsequent events make us wonder if the invitation was sincere or just another attempt to set a trap for the Savior

II. **A Daring Intrusion**
    A. In the midst of the meal, a woman breaks into the scene
    B. She is both a welcome and an unwelcome intruder
        1. It is obvious that Jesus was glad to see her
        2. Simon surely could have done without her visit
    C. She takes some really unusual action
        1. Washes His feet with her tears (of repentance or gratitude)
        2. Pours expensive perfume on Him

III. **Question and Answer Time**
    A. We see a Pharisee talking to himself
        1. If this man knew who she really is, He wouldn't let her touch Him
        2. He formed a judgment based on appearances
    B. He got answers he wasn't looking for
        1. You don't know her, but I know you!
        2. Let me tell you about yourself

IV. **A Telling Tale**
    A. The tables are turned
        1. You showed me no welcome; she cared for what you should have done
        2. She demonstrates that she has been forgiven much; you show little or nothing in that regard
    B. A man caught in his own trap

        1. He set himself up without even realizing he was doing so

        2. This is not all that uncommon with Jesus

V. An Appropriate Application

  A. Her twofold declaration

      1. She was declaring that Jesus was someone special

      2. She was expressing her mixed sorrow for what she had done and her gratitude for what He had done

  B. His utter insensitivity

      1. Simon was incapable of seeing his own failure and shortcomings

      2. He had no interest in finding forgiveness because he didn't know he needed it

  C. This is a clear instance of "only a sinner, saved by grace!"

VI. A Divine Design

Jesus had some things to say about . . .

  A. The subtle appeal of self-righteousness

  B. The extravagant nature of gratitude

  C. Which is it? Much or little?

Conclusion:

A sinful woman demonstrates the fullness of gratitude for grace. A self-righteous Pharisee is offended by all this. To what degree are you grateful, or to what degree has self-righteousness blunted that gratitude? Do you demonstrate gratitude or subtly criticize the "excesses" of those who do?

The Conversation with a "Rich Young Ruler"

Matthew 19:16–30; Mark 10:17–31; Luke 18:18–30

Introduction:

In a materialistic society like ours, a conversation between Jesus and a rich man has to be of interest to many. Jesus actually answers our frequent question: "Is it wrong to be rich?" He does so by pointing out a major principle for a determination on the subject.

I. **The Sincerely Insincere**
    A. He seems sincerely interested in spiritual things
    B. He asks the wrong question when he uses the word "do"
    C. It appears that he is looking for a vindication of his trust in good works and in riches

II. **A Wrong Assumption Begets an Inaccurate Question**
    A. His focus is on "do" where so many manage to keep their focus
    B. Jesus makes a summary statement: if I am good, then I am God
    C. Jesus quotes the second half of the Ten Commandments. Why?
        1. The young man would likely claim some form of perfection regarding the first four commandments
        2. His real problem lay in the area of his relationship to others (which showed that he actually had other gods before God)

III. **A Revealing Presumption**
    He said "All these things have I kept from my youth."
    A. Note that Jesus does not challenge him directly on this
    B. What Jesus does is make him recognize his own failure

IV. **Jesus Goes to the Point and at the Heart**
    A. His request corrects the wrong assumptions of the man
        1. Jesus shows him what his priorities really are
        2. Jesus brings him to see his own problem
    B. He hits the man where it really hurts
        1. Giving all away would not save him; it would demonstrate his understanding of what Jesus was all about
        2. He failed the test

C. He creates a double sorrow
   1. The man goes away sorrowful
   2. Jesus watches with sorrow as he goes away

V. A Camel and the Eye of a Needle: A rich man and heaven
   A. Is it wrong to have riches?
      1. Not really
      2. It all depends on one's view of them
   B. Then what's wrong with them?
      1. They tend to capture the affections
      2. They promote self-satisfaction
      3. They produce the pride that often eschews identification with Jesus
      4. They consume the time necessary to develop spiritual relationships
      5. They become a source of security
      6. They tempt us to things that are wrong in the process of securing them

VI. And What About Us?
   A. The disciples didn't have much, but the "have-nots" can be equally materialistic
   B. And modern Americans?
      1. We have so much
      2. We face grave danger through that which we possess

Conclusion:

Is it wrong to be rich? The answer depends on several factors. Do we recognize the source of our riches? Are we willing to use our riches to advance His kingdom and help others? What do our riches mean to us? It is a question that only you can answer.